THE HOLOCAUST

HOLOCAUSTS IN OTHER LANDS

Stuart A. Kallen

Published by Abdo & Daughters, 4940 Viking Drive, Suite 622, Edina, Minnesota 55435.

Library bound edition distributed by Rockbottom Books, Pentagon Tower, P.O. Box 36036, Minneapolis, Minnesota 55435.

Cover Photo credit: Bettmann Archives
Interior Photo credits: Sygma, pages 39, 41, 43
                   Bettmann Archives, pages 9, 13, 15, 32, 34, 36,
                   Archives photos, pages 11, 17, 20, 21, 23

Edited by Rosemary Wallner

Library of Congress Cataloging-in-Publication Data

Kallen, Stuart A., 1955—
      Holocausts in other lands / Stuart A. Kallen.
           p.   cm. -- (The Holocaust)
      Includes bibliographical references and index.
      ISBN 1-56239-355-3
      1. Genocide--History--Juvenile literature. [1. Genocide.]
    I. Title. II. Series: Holocaust (Edina, Minn.)
HV6322.7.K35   1994
304.6'63'09--dc20
                                          94-5378
                                             CIP
                                             AC

Table of Contents

Foreword 4

Is the Holocaust Unique? 5

A New Term for an Old Crime 8

How Genocide Happens 10

When Genocide Happens 12

Native American Genocide 14

The African Holocaust 19

The Armenians 22

The Ukraine: Starvation for Ideology 25

The Gypsies: Hitlers Other Victims 26

After World War II 28

Tibet: An Ancient Culture Under Siege 29

East Timor: The Hidden Genocide 31

Cambodia: Millions Forced From Their Cities 32

Bosnia: Ethnic Cleansing 35

Rwanda: The Tribal Killing Fields 38

Final Word 42

Glossary 44

Bibliography 45

Index 46

FOREWORD

The Holocaust is a tragic time in world history. It was a time of prejudice and bias turned to hate and the persecution of an ethnic group by persons who came into a position of power, allowing them to carry out that hate.

The Holocaust series depicts what prejudice and biases can lead to; how men, women and children—simply because they were Jewish—died horrible deaths.

When a child is born it has no prejudices. Bias must be learned and someone has to display it.

The goal of this series is to enlighten children and help them recognize the ignorance of prejudice so that future generations will be tolerant, understanding, compassionate, and free of prejudice.

Acknowledgments:

Rabbi Morris Allen
        Beth Jacob Congregation

Dr. Stewart Ross
        Mankato State University

Special Thanks to The United States Holocaust Memorial Museum

CHAPTER ONE

IS THE HOLOCAUST UNIQUE?

*I*n 1945 the ugly truth was out about Nazi Germany's so-called "Final Solution to the Jewish Problem." It was first witnessed when soldiers liberated the concentration camps. Later it was spelled out in sickening detail at the Nuremberg Trials. The entire world gasped in horror at the Nazi crimes against humanity.

The Nazis had used the power of the government to outlaw the very existence of an entire race of people—the Jewish people. After they were outlawed, they were rounded up, arrested, and deported in cattle cars on trains to death camps. Once at the camps, Jewish men, women, and children were exterminated in gas chambers by the millions. When they were dead, their bodies were burned in ovens called crematoria.

The Nazis used the technology of the time to run the death camps efficiently. They ran the camps at a profit, using slave-labor to run German industry at wartime levels. The Nazis broke all bounds of human decency by shaving the heads of the victims and using the hair for clothing. They also pulled the gold teeth from the corpses and melted them down into gold bars for the German treasury.

When the Nazis were done, they had killed 70 percent of the Jewish men, women, and children living in Europe. In some countries like Poland, they killed 90 percent of the Jews. All together, this amounted to 6 million people. Most of them were killed in a time span of only five years, from 1940 to 1945. This event in history became known as the Holocaust.

Millions of others were killed in World War II, and many millions died in the same death camps as the Jews. Gypsies, Jehovah's Witnesses, trade unionists, Communists, and homosexuals were all ordered to their deaths in Nazi gas chambers.

Is it possible to measure human evil? Is it less terrible to kill six hundred people than to kill six million? Is it more evil to kill people in gas chambers than to bomb their city? Is it worse to destroy people through slavery than to wipe them off the face of the earth? These are the types of questions that arise when discussing the Holocaust.

Sadly, history is full of horrors. There is no way to compare one person's suffering with another's. How then is the murder of 6 million Jewish people different?

The answer may be found in the words of German historian Eberhard Jäckel. He stated:

Never before had any state, with all the authority of its responsible leader, decided and announced that it intended to kill off a particular group of human beings, including the old, the women, and children, the suckling babies, as completely as possible, and had then translated this decision into action with every possible power at the state's command.

American historian Lucy S. Dawidowicz added to that answer. She wrote:

In every case of terrible human destructiveness that we have known...killing was not an end in itself, but a means to an end... But in the murder of the European Jews, ends and means were identical.

What Dawidowicz meant is that in other times groups of people were murdered for their land, or their riches, or because they had something that the murderers wanted. But the European Jews had very little land or power. In fact the Nazis were murdering them in countries that they already conquered in war. The only reason they were killing the Jews was to wipe them off the face of the earth.

It has also been said that the Nazis might have succeeded in taking over Europe for a longer time if they had not spent so much time, energy, and resources killing the Jews. Even when they knew they were losing the war, they continued to murder Jews.

CHAPTER TWO

A NEW TERM FOR AN OLD CRIME

*G*enocide is defined by the dictionary as "the systematic extermination of a national or racial group." Before 1944, the word did not exist. It was coined in the worst year of the Holocaust by a Polish legal scholar, Raphael Lemkin. He created the word to describe what was happening to the Jewish people in Nazi-occupied Europe.

Lemkin combined the Greek word genos (nation, tribe) with the Latin suffix -cide (killing). He felt the word was needed as a legal term that would accurately describe the deliberate killing of an entire human group. Lemkin later promoted treaties at the United Nations to make genocide illegal. It became international law in 1948.

Genocide is a new word for an ancient crime. The Bible has many stories about groups of people being slaughtered. Joshua (1200 B.C.) and a series of judges and warriors led the Israelites on the invasion and gradual occupation of Canaan, the Promised Land. In the eighth and seventh centuries B.C., Assyrians in southwest Asia burned cities to the ground and exterminated whole populations. The Romans did the same in Carthage in 146 B.C. As a matter of fact, massacres of whole groups of people were the order of the day in ancient times.

In the Middle Ages (A.D. 500 to 1500) wars of religion were waged. They were a major feature of ancient history and are still with us today. Religious wars cause people of one religion to justify murder because the victims have different beliefs.

The Christian Crusades began in 1099 and continued for hundreds of years. During the Crusades, innocent Jews and Muslims were killed in large numbers. During the Inquisition, begun in 1492, the Spanish Roman Catholic church allowed mass murder of nonbelievers, including many Jews. Many of the excuses for this murder were revived by the Nazis centuries later. Religious wars have affected many people from Europe to Africa to the Middle East to China. As a matter of fact, religion usually plays a central role in one group's genocide against another.

The Crusades' European armies invaded the Middle East to Christianize it.

CHAPTER THREE

HOW GENOCIDE HAPPENS

*G*enocide can be defined by three parts that make up a whole: ideology, technology, and bureaucracy.

Ideology. Ideology (i-de-OL-e-je) is a set of ideas and beliefs that guide a person, group, or nation. Some ideologies are good and help people, such as belief in charity and kindness. But some ideologies are bad and hurtful. Nazism and racism are thought of as bad ideologies.

A key element of genocide is an ideology that allows the murderers to excuse murder. The ideology of genocide is usually based on racist or religious beliefs. Information or ideas are repeated over and over to change the public's thinking about a group of people. This is called propaganda. Such propaganda defines the victims as not worthy of human kindness or sympathy. Words such as "savages," "vermin," "sub-human," and "non-believers" are used to define the victims. Racist terms are also used. Once a group of people are reduced to a non-human level in the minds of the majority, the victims are easier to kill. Racist ideologies may survive for thousands of years, so that the victims are naturally thought of as inferior and useless by large numbers of people.

Technology. Once propaganda separates and labels the victim "non-human," the killing can begin. As the world has become a more modern place, people have developed more modern means of murder. In ancient times, clubs, spears, and guns were the means of mass murder. The Nazis used high-tech methods such as gas chambers and crematoria. Today, we have "smart" bombs and nuclear bombs that can do the work of mass human annihilation in minutes.

Bureaucracy. Most governments are made up of hundreds of departments, cabinets, administrators, and bureaus. Taken together they are called a bureaucracy (byur-OK-re-see).

When a group decides to commit genocide it needs more than an army to do the killing. Laws must be passed to declare the victims enemies of the state. Prisons and concentration camps must be built. Courts must give trials to people who resist. Generals, lieutenants, sergeants, and soldiers must receive marching orders. Businesses must be contracted to build weapons, clothing, and machinery. All of these things require a bureaucracy to write papers, file documents, and give orders. The German genocide of the Jews and Gypsies required an enormous bureaucracy to coordinate the efforts.

Jewish victims in the Warsaw ghetto during World War II.

CHAPTER FOUR

WHEN GENOCIDE HAPPENS

*G*enocide has usually taken place under three conditions—war, colonization, and religious or tribal conflict.

War. Wartime conditions are especially favorable for genocide. When armies are fighting each other, genocide and violent acts against citizens are thought of as a continuation of the warfare. Wartime also allows the censorship of ideas and the use of propaganda on a massive scale. The enemy is labeled as inhuman. People who oppose the killing are called traitors.

Colonization. When one nation forms a colony in another, it is called colonization (kol-e-niz-A-shun). This happened when Spain, England, and France sent thousands of people to America. Those Europeans colonized America, taking away the power of the Native Americans who already lived there. Colonization has led to the genocide among native peoples from North and South America to New Zealand and Australia. It is still happening in the rain forests of Brazil and elsewhere.

Religious or Tribal Conflict. The third arena for genocide is conflict of one religion or tribe against another. Modern-day examples of this type of genocide may be found in the Eastern European countries of Boznia and the African country of Rwanda.

250,000 Rwanda refugees cross the border into Tanzania from Rwanda with all their belongings. Tribal fighting has been the cause of much suffering within the densely populated African country of Rwanda.

CHAPTER FIVE

NATIVE AMERICAN GENOCIDE

*M*any people believe that the native peoples of the Americas have suffered the worst genocide of any people in history. They were stripped of their culture, land, natural resources, and their very lives. As wave after wave of Europeans came to America, Native Americans were forced off their land.

Fifty years after Christopher Columbus landed in the Bahamas, the natives who lived there, the Arawaks, were extinct. The Spanish colonists used the Arawaks as slaves and worked them until they dropped.

The Spanish invaded the Americas with a vengeance. In 1519 Hernando Cortéz invaded the Aztec city of Tenochtitlán. The city was far more dazzling than any in Europe. The city had five times the population of London, England. In two years, over 350,000 Aztecs were murdered. The entire Aztec empire contained over 25 million people. That was five times the population of England. After 75 years of Spanish rule only 1 million Aztecs were left alive.

The Spaniards were unbelievably cruel. They worked the natives to death in mines, chained together at the neck.

The ancient Aztec ruins. These pyramids are located about 40 miles from Mexico City.

In Central America, 95 percent of the native people were either killed or died from European diseases that they had no resistance to. In Nicaragua, 99 percent of the natives were killed—more than one million people—in only 60 years. In Peru and Chile, 14 million native people died. In all, it is estimated that 80 to 90 million people from the Indies to the Amazon died before the dawning of the seventeenth century. Some of the population collapse was due to disease introduced by the Europeans.

Although the Spanish killed millions, they still valued the natives as slave labor. The same cannot be said of the English who landed in North America.

Scientists do not agree on exactly how many Native Americans lived in North America before the English arrived. Estimates range from a low of 7 million to a high of 30 million. There is no doubt, however, that at the beginning of the twentieth century, only 250,000 remained. That means that 97 to 99 percent of Native Americans were killed or died between 1620 and 1900.

The English who settled America in the early 1600s did not find gold or silver. But with a population explosion occurring in the British Isles, they needed more land. Since the Native Americans stood in the way of unlimited access to North America, they had to be eliminated. So they were.

In Virginia the English burned entire native villages and the surrounding cornfields. They poisoned whole communities with blankets infected with small pox disease. They captured women and children and sold them as slaves in West India. Within 50 years, Virginia's natives were gone, reduced to 1,500 people from 100,000.

This pattern was repeated throughout New England. By the early 1800s, 95 percent of the Native Americans were killed. This genocide took place in the span of 100 years. In 1703, Massachusetts law gave people the right to shoot "Indians."

After the American Revolution, the new nation supported Native American genocide. Andrew Jackson, whose picture graces the ten dollar bill, called Native Americans "savage dogs." At one time, Jackson supervised the slaughter of 800 members of the Creek tribe. The soldiers cut off the noses of the dead and made bridle reins out of strips of Native American's skin.

Native American Indian chief Geronimo suffered through the resettlement march known as the "Trail of Tears."

After Jackson became president, the U. S. Congress passed the Indian Removal Act in 1830. The act ordered Native Americans to be resettled in the west. Thousands upon thousands of Native Americans were rounded up in the southeast and southwest United States. The government seized their land and forced them to march to Kansas, Nebraska, and Oklahoma.

The U. S. army oversaw the march, which became known as the "Trail of Tears." Unaccustomed to the cold, hundreds froze to death. Others died of starvation. Many died from disease. Natives from the Cherokee, Creek, Seminole, Shawnee, Wyandot, Chickasaw, and Choctaw tribes died by the thousands. By the time the Native Americans were forced onto arid, barren reservations, thousands were dead or dying.

The genocide of the Native Americans lasted for four hundred years. People from the countries of England, France, Spain, Portugal, the Netherlands, and Germany participated in the massacre. The U. S. government gave specific orders to take the wealth of the Native Americans, steal their land, and send them to reservations.

By the 1890s the native population of the United States had dropped to 1 percent of its former number. The languages, medicines, artwork, music, and knowledge of hundreds of rich and exciting cultures was gone forever.

The annihilation of the native peoples of America continues. During the 1980s over 10,000 natives were murdered in Guatemala. Native people are being wiped out in the rain forests of Brazil. And many of the Native Americans in the United States are poor and suffering from four hundred years of genocide.

CHAPTER SIX

THE AFRICAN HOLOCAUST

*A*fter the Europeans discovered America, they quickly set about to plunder its natural resources. There were seas to fish, forests to cut, crops to plant, and precious metals to mine. Unfortunately, Europeans were not used to this hard labor. At first they tried to enslave Native Americans. But most of the natives chose to lay down and die rather than be slaves for the European conquerors.

As the Europeans sailed their ships to America, they passed the continent of Africa. Africa was a vast, rich land full of hundreds of cultures and millions of people. In Ghana people worked with iron and gold. In Mali thousands of traders crisscrossed the country in caravans led by camels. In Timbuktu mosques were laid out with velvet, fountains, and artwork carved into stone. In present-day Nigeria craft workers made incredible artwork out of brass. Africa was alive with music, dance, art, and knowledge from thousands of tribal cultures.

All that was to change. First the Portuguese, then other nations, began to plunder Africa for human slaves. The first Africans came to the New World not as slaves but as sailors. There were Africans traveling with Balboa when he became the first European to see the Pacific Ocean. There were Africans with Hernando Cortéz in Peru in the 1500s. Some historians believe that there was an African traveling with Columbus in 1492.

In 1620 the first Africans were brought to America to slave in the tobacco fields in Virginia. Soon the trickle of slaves turned into a flood.

The Spanish, Portuguese, French, English, Dutch, and Danish all fought with each other to see who would dominate the slave trade. The English finally became the masters of the sea and the masters of the slave trade in 1713.

An English slave ship bringing Africans to the Americas.

By the early eighteenth century, Europeans were kidnapping 80,000 Africans a year and bringing them to America for slavery. Slavers called their human cargo "Black Gold." Huge companies were set up whose only purpose was to make slaves out of free Africans—more bureaucracy in action. Propaganda was printed to paint a picture of the Africans as savage, backward, and less than human. The accomplishments of African civilization were hidden from the public.

Conditions aboard the slave ships were horrible. Small sailing vessels were packed with as many as 400 human beings. Families were broken apart. Slaves were chained together at the wrists and ankles. Each male was given a space 6 feet long and 16 inches high aboard the ship. Women and children were given less space. The journey took endless weeks. The Africans were forced to live in filth. Sea sickness, suicide, and disease killed about two-thirds of the unfortunate people.

No one knows exactly how many Africans were kidnapped and brought to America. Some historians believe that at least 50 million people were taken from Africa—about half of all people living there. Of that number, possibly 35 million died or were killed along the way.

The continent of Africa was left in ruins. Great libraries and universities were destroyed. Over 500 separate languages were lost. Cities were abandoned and returned to dust.

American human slavery lasted for almost three hundred years. Even after slavery was outlawed after the Civil War, African-Americans were still treated like aliens in their own land. Propaganda and bureaucracy continued to work against their well-being. The legacy of the African Holocaust is still with us today.

African-American slaves in the 1800s working in a cotton field.

CHAPTER SEVEN

THE ARMENIANS

*I*n 1939 on the eve of World War II, Adolf Hitler silenced some of his generals who were having doubts about the planned mass murder of the Jews and others. Hitler said, "Who, after all, speaks today of the annihilation of the Armenians?...The world believes in success alone."

Unfortunately, the Armenian genocide has been overlooked by history. It was completely forgotten during Hitler's era and it is still not well-known today. This is because the mass murders happened during wartime (World War I). It is also because of the propaganda put out by the Turkish murderers who were responsible.

In the late years of the nineteenth century, there was an independence movement started among the 2.5 million Christian Armenians in Muslim Turkey. In 1894 there was a massacre of Armenian men, women, and children. There was another large killing in 1909.

By 1915 Turkey was afraid the Armenians would help their Russian enemies during World War I. The Armenians were ordered out of Turkey and deported forcibly to Palestine and Syria. The Turkish government did little to hide what the deportations really meant—mass slaughter of innocent people.

The Turkish Army and police first rounded up all the educated Armenians and killed them. Writers, poets, lawyers, doctors, merchants, bankers, and the wealthy were gunned down.

Joseph Goebbels (L), Nazi Minister of propaganda, with Adolf Hitler,
the leader of Germany's Nazi party.

After killing the Armenian leaders, the Turks then went from town to town and killed able-bodied Armenian men.

There was a common pattern for the deportations. It would start with a town crier saying that all Armenian men should report to the local government building. When the men arrived, they were thrown, without reason, into prison. After being jailed a day or two, the men would be roped together and marched out of town to a lonely spot. Then they were massacred.

The remaining old men, women, and children were marched, across hundreds of miles of barren mountains and desert. Some were tied together with ropes. They died by the tens of thousands of thirst, starvation, and disease. People who could not keep up with the march were bayoneted or shot.

Once they were marched into the desert, the remaining Armenians were simply left to die in the barren wastelands. Local Muslim peasants carried off the remaining women while their babies were left to die.

All remnants of Armenian Christian culture were destroyed. Homes were ransacked. Churches were burned.

When it was over, the Turkish Armenian population of 1.8 million had been reduced to about 32,500. Hitler and the Nazis learned the Turkish method of mass slaughter. They used some of those methods on Jewish men, women, and children 20 years later. Of course the Nazis went beyond the crude Turkish methods and were able to slaughter millions more people in an efficient and cold-blooded manner. But the Turks showed the world that genocide was possible at new levels as the world settled into the twentieth century.

CHAPTER EIGHT

THE UKRAINE: STARVATION FOR IDEOLOGY

*T*he Ukraine was a state in the United Soviet Socialist Republic (USSR). It is and was a major source of grain for the Soviet Union. In the 1930s, Soviet Premier Joseph Stalin ordered the Ukrainians to give up their land to the state. The state would run the farms and the owners would simply become workers for the state. The fiercely independent Ukrainians resisted the government coming in and taking away their hard-earned property rights.

Stalin reacted by sending his secret police to take the Ukrainian farms by force. The police were nothing but a roaming gang of thugs. They stole everything they could. They took shoes off of children and warm clothes off adults. The police killed thousands of people. Stalin had planned to take the farms from 6 million people. The police gladly raised that number to 10 million.

As a punishment to weaken further resistance, Stalin ordered all Ukrainian grain to be shipped from the area and none to be brought in. Millions began to starve. People ate mice, worms, tree bark, and old shoes. Human flesh sold in the market. Stalin stockpiled the food and surrounded it by armed guards. People starved as potatoes rotted surrounded by barbed wire and soldiers.

It is estimated that 5 million Ukrainians died by Stalin's manmade famine. Three million died between 1932-1933 alone. In other parts of the country 20 million others died because no food came out of the Ukrainian region.

(Once the government seized the farms, no one knew how to run them.) Soviet agriculture was destroyed and it did not recover for decades. This explains why, when the Nazis invaded the Ukraine, they were welcomed with open arms.

CHAPTER NINE

THE GYPSIES: HITLER'S OTHER VICTIMS

The Gypsies, or Rom, as they wish to be called, are also members of a forgotten genocide. They have a rich oral history, but few writers have documented their destruction.

The original home of Gypsies was in Northern India. Scientists believe that the Gypsies are pure descendants of the original Aryans, the people who first settled Germany. This is ironic since Hitler killed the Gypsies while claiming to purify the world for the Aryan race.

The Gypsies left their home two thousand years ago and became wandering nomads. By the fifteenth century, Gypsies could be found in Persia, Germany, Austria, Italy, and other central European countries. The Gypsies were poor wanderers and depended on fortune telling, music, dancing, and handicrafts to make a living. Because of their lower status, some depended on stealing farm animals and crops for food. Because of this, Gypsies were shunned in most countries and forbidden from entering.

Gypsies were subject to periodic mass killings. They were forced to leave many countries.

The only place they were tolerated was in the Balkan countries such as Romania, Bulgaria, and Albania. But by the nineteenth century, the Gypsies were given more freedom and allowed to travel freely through Europe. Germany and Austria were the only countries that refused to allow Gypsies entry.

Because the Gypsies were nomads, it is impossible to determine their numbers on the eve of World War II. Best guesses are that there were 1.4 million Gypsies in Europe.

The Nazis took their racial purity very seriously. They considered Germans to be a pure race of Aryans—the only people capable of ruling the world. The poor cousins of the Aryans—the Gypsies—were an embarrassment to Hitler. He ordered his scientists to say that the Gypsies were non-Aryan. They did as they were told. Those who disagreed were sent to concentration camps. To be declared an alien to the Aryan race was a death sentence in Nazi-occupied Europe.

Hitler's propaganda called the Gypsies "parasites on the body of our people," and "a danger to the racial purity of our peasants," and "confirmed criminals." At first, Hitler ordered sterilization of the Gypsies and their deportment for slave labor.

After 1940 the cover of World War II allowed the Nazis to go further. Hitler deported 30,000 Gypsies to the concentration camps of Poland, along with as many Jews. In 1941, the commander of Nazi-occupied Serbia ordered that all property of Gypsies and Jews be taken from them. The Gypsies were deported to Jewish ghettos. Next a huge trial was held in Slovakia, in which the entire race of Gypsies was declared to be cannibals—eaters of human flesh. So, using ridiculous propaganda and bureaucracy, Hitler condemned an entire race to death.

Gypsies were herded into special sections of Jewish ghettos. German soldiers took particular glee in the drunken torture of Gypsies. Thousands died from beatings and typhus. There were more than 100,000 Gypsies in the Warsaw ghetto alone.

Because the Gypsies were used to wandering, they were harder to round up than the mostly urban Jews. Some Gypsies were able to escape the Holocaust because local officials were willing to look the other way. That was something they rarely did in the case of the Jews. There are even stories of Gypsies helping Jews to escape the Nazis.

Still, a huge percentage of Gypsies were exterminated by the Nazis. In Germany, 9 out of 10 were killed. In Latvia almost all died. In Croatia, only 1 percent lived. In all, at least 500,000 Gypsies died in the Holocaust. That is about one-third their total number. The Jews lost two-thirds their total number, but the Gypsies were second in the horrible tally of Nazi mass-murder.

CHAPTER TEN

AFTER WORLD WAR II

*T*he world stood in shock when it realized the mass murders conducted by the German Nazis during World War II. People could not believe the scope or the brutality in which the atrocities were carried out. Bills outlawing genocide were introduced into the United Nations and quickly ratified by many countries.

Since World War II, there have been at least ten incidences of genocide in the world. They were in isolated areas around the globe in places such as Africa, Asia, and South America. They have been given very little press coverage in the United States. Most people have never even heard of East Timor or Burundi. Other genocides, like Cambodia and Tibet, have been given a little more coverage, but still remain vague to people. Most people feel that little can be done to stop the killing. Some even refuse to call it genocide. They prefer "internal conflict" or other terms.

CHAPTER ELEVEN

TIBET: AN ANCIENT CULTURE UNDER SIEGE

*T*he Buddhist religion has ruled life in Tibet for centuries. Until the 1960s at least one out of every six Tibetan males was either a Buddhist priest or monk. All religious and political leaders were priests. Communist China invaded Tibet in 1959, bringing strict Communist philosophy to the beautiful mountainous country. The spiritual leader of Tibet, the Dalai Lama, was forced to flee his homeland.

The Chinese government brought over 1 million Chinese natives into Tibet, in addition to 300,000 soldiers. As a result, the Chinese began to outnumber the Tibetans in their own homeland.

It is estimated that over 1 million Tibetans lost their lives under Chinese rule. Others were imprisoned or forced to work as slave labor.

Widespread crop failures resulted from the Chinese ordering the Tibetans to grow wheat and rice instead of the hardy barley they used to grow. Tibetans starved while their harvests were shipped to feed the Chinese.

Saddest of all, the Tibetans were forced to deny their beautiful culture. The Chinese forbid them to speak their own language or practice their religion. Masterpieces of Tibetan artwork were destroyed. Statues were smashed and ancient temples were used for grain storage. The Chinese government did everything it could to destroy the Tibetan ways and replace them with Chinese customs. In a few years, Tibetan culture was almost completely lost.

Today, Tibetans live as second-class citizens in their own land. China, meanwhile, is becoming a major economic force in Asia. Trading partners such as the United States do not mention Tibet to Chinese leaders for fear of losing business relations with China. The Dalai Lama, meanwhile, travels the world telling people not to forget Tibet. He hopes to return to his homeland one day after it has been freed of Chinese Communist repression.

CHAPTER TWELVE

EAST TIMOR:
THE HIDDEN GENOCIDE

*T*he East Indies island of East Timor is located about 350 miles from Australia. Portugal ruled the eastern half of the island for four hundred years. The Dutch ruled the western half. After World War II, the Indonesian Republic was formed out of the islands that had been the Netherlands East Indies. East Timor, however, remained a Portuguese colony. Because of its isolation, East Timor remained different ethnically than the other islands of Indonesia.

In 1974 East Timor overthrew its Portuguese rulers. But in 1975 Indonesia stepped in to deny the people of East Timor their freedom. Although the Indonesian government denies it, reports smuggled out of the country show that over 200,000 East Timorese have died since the 1975 invasion. Most of the survivors have been forced into "resettlement camps." There, starvation was common. At least another 25,000 died in the camps. In a land that once supported 690,000 people, this mass murder is more than one of every three people. This is the largest percentage of a group of people being slaughtered since the Holocaust.

In the 1990s, the repression of East Timor continues. In 1991 Indonesian troops killed 271 peaceful protesters with machine guns. For now, the surviving people of East Timor can only hope that the world takes notice of their plight.

CHAPTER THIRTEEN

CAMBODIA: MILLIONS FORCED FROM THEIR CITIES

*C*ambodia is a small country near Vietnam in Southeast Asia. Khmer Rouge communists took over the country in 1975. At the time, the Khmer Rouge had been fighting a civil war in Cambodia for five years. They were fighting the U.S. backed government.

Cambodian soldiers examine the bones of soldiers and villagers found after government forces recaptured a highway about 60 miles northwest of Phnom Penh.

The Khmer Rouge soldiers swarmed into the Cambodian capital of Phnom Penh. They ordered the 3 million people there to abandon the city. Young and old, sick and healthy, businesspeople and beggars, all were ordered at gunpoint onto the streets and highways.

The hospitals were emptied of the sick and dying. They too were forced to stumble out of the city. Those who were too sick to walk were pushed in their beds by members of their families. Doctors were forced to abandon their patients in mid-operation. It took two full days to empty the city.

Thousands died in the forced march. The weak were quickly executed. Phnom Penh was not alone. The entire urban population of Cambodia, some 4 million people, were forced from the cities. It was one of the largest transfers of human beings in history.

The survivors were settled in villages and agricultural communes in the Cambodian countryside. They were put to work for 17 hours a day. They planted rice and built irrigation systems.

Many thousands died from dysentery, malaria, and starvation. They were given one can of condensed milk and one bowl of rice every two days. Others were taken away in the night by the Khmer Rouge and shot.

All educated people were killed. Anyone who wore eyeglasses was killed. Musicians and artists skilled in ancient tradition were killed. Buddhism, the major religion, was outlawed. Ancient temples, thousands of years old, were destroyed. There were no telephones, no public transportation, no postal service, and no schools or universities. Phnom Penh became a ghost town of shuttered shops, abandoned offices, and painted-over street signs.

The Vietnamese-installed Cambodian government maintains an exhibition of skulls and bones at a mass gravesite outside Phnom Penh, Cambodia, to demonstrate the cruelty of Pol Pot's Khmer Rouge regime, which was ousted by Vietnamese soldiers in 1979.

The leader of the Khmer Rouge was Pol Pot. His Communist ideology stated that money was the root of all evil. Pol Pot decided to abolish money. And where was the money? In the cities. Pol Pot didn't care that millions would die for his ideology. When asked about the millions who died, one minister of the government said, "It's amazing how concerned you Westerners are about war criminals." Pol Pot even boasted about his destruction, saying, "More than 2,000 years of Cambodian history have virtually ended."

This mass murder was largely ignored in the West. The United States had just pulled out of Vietnam. They certainly weren't about to return to Cambodia to stop Pol Pot. The United Nations even refused to name what the Khmer Rouge was doing as genocide.

In 1993, Cambodia's 70-year-old King Sihanouk returned to rule the country after living in exile since 1955. It is hoped that the king, and his son who is prime minister, can return Cambodia to its former glory.

CHAPTER FOURTEEN

BOSNIA: ETHNIC CLEANSING

The Balkans—Bosnia, Serbia, and Croatia—have long been a firecracker in world politics. It was in the Balkans where the spark that started World War I was set off. During World War II some of the worst atrocities were committed in the Balkans. The Croats backed the Nazis and the Serbs backed the Soviet Union. After World War II, the region was called Yugoslavia. The Soviet Union imposed a long truce after the war.

An old Muslim woman reads the Koran (holy book) in front of the grave of her son, a Bosnian defender.

Two women try to identify the remnants of a missing relative after gaining access to a mass grave in the Baltic republic of Lithuanian.

In 1990 when the Soviet Union collapsed, old hatreds returned to the region. The Serbs are Orthodox Christians. The Croats are Roman Catholics. Many of the people living in the area are Muslims. All these religions have had conflict with each other in the past.

In 1991 Serbian forces began "ethnic cleansing" in Bosnia and the Herzegovenia region. The Serbs drove more than 1 million Muslims and Croats from their homes. They tortured and killed some, abused and terrorized the rest. Some Muslims and Croats struck back with atrocities of their own. Soon the results began to show up on televisions and in newspapers across the world.

The struggle in the former Yugoslavia became a struggle of one group to "purify" the land by driving out the others. Serbs set up death camps where Muslims and Croats were kept in conditions similar to the Nazi concentration camps of World War II.

As the world stood by and watched, a new era of genocidal cruelty began in Yugoslavia. Once again the Balkans may have provided the spark for conflicts engulfing millions of Europeans.

CHAPTER FIFTEEN

RWANDA: THE TRIBAL KILLING FIELDS

*E*uropeans who came to Rwanda one hundred years ago found a country ruled by tall, thin, Tutsi cattle lords who obeyed a mystical Tutsi king. Darker-skinned, stockier Hutus farmed the land and kept the Tutsis clothed and fed. The country was about 15 percent Tutsis and 85 percent Hutus. Although the Tutsis were outnumbered they ruled the country. Both tribes lived in harmony.

But the Germans colonized Rwanda. After World War I, the Belgians ruled Rwanda from faraway Europe. The Belgians left the Tutsis in charge of the country. The Tutsis were given educations. A minimum height requirement was set for the sons of chiefs who wanted to go to school. This disqualified the shorter Hutus. The Tutsis received the best jobs and the Belgians drained the wealth from the tiny nation. That created great rifts between the two native groups.

The years of colonialism destroyed the social and political structure that had kept the peace for hundreds of years. By 1959 the Hutu majority rose up in rebellion. In some villages, machete-wielding gangs set upon Tutsis and hacked off their feet to make them shorter. Seeing that the Hutus would win, the Belgians quickly sided with them, abandoning their Tutsi allies. All the while the population of the tiny country kept growing, making land and water scarce.

Tutsi refugees after being driven out of their homeland of Rwanda.

Tutsi victims stacked up on a beach in Rwanda.

In 1962, the Belgians granted independence to Rwanda. The Hutus took the opportunity to strike back at the Tutsis. All Rwandans were forced to carry ethnic-identity cards. There was talk of herding all the Tutsis into certain regions. There was widespread murder of Tutsis.

In 1972 the conflict between the Hutus and the Tutsis spread through Burundi, the country south of Rwanda. Hutus armed with machetes and machine guns murdered 100,000 Tutsis. This was in a population of 3.5 million in Burundi. This would be comparable to the United States losing 8 million people.

On April 6, 1994, an airplane carrying the leader of Rwanda and the leader of Burundi was shot down in Rwanda. The two leaders had been trying to negotiate a peace between the Tutsis and the Hutus. With the death of the leaders, massacres began once again.

The Hutus instantly blamed the Tutsis for the death of Rwanda's leader. Within minutes, Hutu soldiers took to the streets along with mobs of drunken young men. They began to hunt down Tutsi civilians, killing them where they stood. Western nations quickly pulled their people out of the country, leaving Rwandans to fend for themselves.

A frenzy of hand-to-hand killing swept through Rwanda. With no water or electricity, people huddled in their homes, listening to the screams of their neighbors as the soldiers found them. Blood flowed down the aisles of churches where Tutsis hid. Toddlers were sliced in half. The rivers ran red with blood and mutilated bodies. Every road in the country was littered with bodies.

An estimate of 100,000 to 500,000 Rwandans were killed within the first month of conflict. No one knows how many died—there were too many to count. In one 24-hour period, over 250,000 Rwandans crossed the border into neighboring Tanzania. This created an instant city, the second largest in the country.

The tragedy in Rwanda shows what can happen when too many people have to battle over soil, water, and other scarce natural resources. This can cause neighbors to kill neighbors. Above all it is an example of ethnic enemies using political conflict to settle scores that date back centuries.

Rwandan children refugees.

CHAPTER SIXTEEN

FINAL WORD

*T*his book could not begin to cover every conflict in the last hundred years where genocide was the rule of the day. Iran, Iraq, El Salvador, Guatamala, Nicaraugua, and other countries have experienced mass killing totaling in the millions.

For the people who want peace in the world, one senseless killing is too much. But those who do not study history, it is said, are doomed to repeat it. So what have we learned?

For one thing, it is harder to hide genocide today. With the invention of the lightweight video camera, millions of people can record what is happening around them. When atrocities are in the public eye, they are harder to ignore. In 1992 the United States invaded Somalia to stop starvation there. Videos and television made the situation there impossible to ignore. This has also been true, to a lesser degree, in Bosnia. Some believe the Jewish Holocaust might have been stopped sooner if the world actually could have seen what was happening.

As we move into a new century, the population of the world continues to grow. It is up to all of us to stop injustice and murder wherever it is happening. For if we don't, who will?

A Tutsi refugee in Rwanda.

GLOSSARY

Annihilate - to reduce to complete ruin, to wipe out completely.

Concentration camp - a guarded camp for the detention and forced labor of political prisoners.

Cremate, crematoria - to cremate is to burn a dead body; this is done in a crematorium; more than one crematorium are crematoria.

Deportation - to expel from a city, region, or country.

Exterminate - to destroy totally.

Ghetto - a section of a city in most European countries where all Jews were forced to live.

Holocaust - the mass extermination of Jews by Nazis.

Nuremberg Trials - Nazi war crime trials held after World War II in Nuremberg, Germany.

Persecute - to harass someone with harsh treatment because of their race, religion, or beliefs.

Persecution - the act of harassing someone with harsh treatment because of their race, religion, or beliefs.

Propaganda - information or ideas that are repeated over and over to change the public's thinking about an idea or group of people.

BIBLIOGRAPHY

Adler, David A. *We Remember the Holocaust.* New York: Henry Holt and Company, 1989.

Aharoni, Yohanan, and Avi-Yonah, Michael. *The Macmillan Bible Atlas.* New York: Macmillan, 1993.

Ausubel, Nathan, and Gross, David C. *Pictorial History of the Jewish People.* New York: Crown Publishers, Inc., 1953, 1984.

Berenbaum, Michael. *The World Must Know.* Boston: Little, Brown and Company, 1993.

Block, Gay, and Drucker. *Malka Rescuers.* New York: Holmes & Meier Publications, Inc., 1992

Chaikin, Miriam A. *Nightmare in History: The Holocaust 1933-1945.* New York: Clarion Books, 1987.

Dawidowicz, Lucy S. *The War Against the Jews 1933-1945.* New York: Seth Press, 1986.

Flannery, Edward H. *The Anguish of the Jews.* New York: Paulist Press, 1985.

Gilbert, Martin. *Final Journey.* New York: Mayflower Books, 1979.

Gilbert, Martin. *The Macmillan Atlas of the Holocaust.* New York: Macmillan, 1982.

Greenfeld, Howard. *The Hidden Children.* New York: Ticknor & Fields, 1993.

Landau, Elaine. *The Warsaw Ghetto Uprising.* New York: New Discovery Books, 1992.

Paldiel, Mordecai. *The Path of the Righteous.* Hoboken, New Jersey: KTAV Publishing House, Inc., 1993.

Index

A

Africa 9, 12, 19,
  20, 21, 29
African-American 21
Albania 27
America 7, 12, 14, 16,
  17, 18, 19, 20, 21,
  29, 32
American Revolution 17
Arawaks 14
Armenians 22, 24
Aryans 26, 27
Asia 8, 29, 30, 32
Assyrian 8
Australia 12, 31
Aztec 14

B

Bahamas 14
Balboa 19
Balkan 27, 35, 37
Bosnia 35, 37, 42
Brazil 12, 18
Buddhist 29
Bulgaria 27
Burundi 29, 40

C

Cambodia 29, 32, 33, 35
Carthage 8
Chile 16
China 9, 29, 30
Columbus, Christopher 14, 19
Communist 6, 29, 30, 32, 35
Cortéz, Hernando 14, 19
crematoria 5, 11
Croatia 28, 35
Crusades 9

D

Dalai Lama 29, 30
death camps 5, 6, 32, 37

E

England 12, 14, 17, 18
Europe 6, 7, 8, 9, 12,
  14, 16, 19, 20, 26, 27,
  37, 38

F

Final Solution 5
France 12, 18

G

gas chambers 5, 6, 11
genocide 8, 9, 10, 11,
  12, 14, 17, 18, 22, 26,
  28, 29, 35, 42
Ghana 19
Gypsies 6, 11, 26, 27, 28

H

Herzegovenia 37
Hitler, Adolf 22, 23, 24, 26, 27
Hutus 38, 40

I

Indian Removal Act 17
Inquisition 9

J

Jackson, Andrew 17

K

Khmer Rouge 32, 33, 35

L

Latvia 28
London 14

M

Mali 19
Middle Ages 8
Muslims 9, 37

N

Native Americans 12, 14,
  16, 17, 18, 19
New Zealand 12
Nicaragua 16
Nigeria 19
nuclear bomb 11
Nuremberg 5

P

Palestine 22
Peru 16, 19
Phnom Penh 33, 34
Pol Pot 35
Poland 6, 27
propaganda 10, 12, 17,
  22, 27

R

Romania 27
Russia 22
Rwanda 12, 38, 40, 41

S

Spain 12, 18
Stalin, Joseph 25
Syria 22

T

Tanzania 41
Tenochtitlán 14
Tibet 29, 30
Timbuktu 19
Timor 29, 31, 32
Turkey 22
Tutsi 38, 40

U

Ukraine 25, 26
United Nations 8, 28, 32, 35
United States 17, 18, 29, 30,
  31, 32, 35, 40, 42
USSR 25

W

Warsaw ghetto 28
World War I 22, 35, 38
World War II 6, 22, 27, 28,
  29, 31, 35, 37

Y

Yugoslavia 35, 37